Authentic, Unapologetic and Real

Erin DeBoer

BookLeaf Publishing

India | USA | UK

Presentation by *BookLeaf Publishing*

Web: www.bookleafpub.com

E-mail: info@bookleafpub.com

ISBN : 9789357447591

First edition 2021

Authentic

I've been so consumed
In my desire
To write something good
That I've forgotten
How to write what is real

I've spent all this time
Shooting for iconic
I think I was trying
To write a prophecy

A sage
An oracle...

Don't put so much
Pressure on yourself
If it's meant to be
You know that it will come
Flow from the pen
Right onto the page
If it should be said
It rolls right off the tongue

Beauty's in the eye of the beholder
A rose can't be picked

Until it's grown
There's no one to look over your shoulder
You can only write
What you have known

Inspiration
Such a funny little thing
It can strike you
In the middle of your sleep
Conversation
Hang your words out on a string
Talk for hours
In the company you keep

The stories that we tell
The message that we sell
Even if it's only me
Who ever knows what I mean

Authentic. Unfiltered. Real.
Express the darkness you feel.
Grateful. Thrilled. The day you arise.
Reflect the sunshine in your eyes.

Paint the color of your mood
Lose the labels "bad" and "good"
Aim instead for something true
And the best thing you can do
Is make it signature you

As A Raindrop

As a raindrop races
Across my window pane,
Consuming one smaller drop,
Then another,
So the desires of life
Keep pulling me in.

I forget
I don't belong to that.

It sounds simple, really.
You tell me I belong to You,
Then send me into the world
Where I'm easily confused.
How do I get off course
Without knowing where I've been?

And I find myself
Here In the same place--
Why can't I stay on track??
I keep asking You
To lead me back.

If I know where my heart is,
It bugs me that I

Can't get my head in the game.
I know I've been drifting
As life pressures me
To throw it all away.

It's easy to say,
"Throw this life to the wind."
Then the winds come up
And I'm tossed around.
No anchor here.
No solid ground.

Still holding on to
A world that breaks my heart.

And all the while,
You've stayed the same.

Put down roots --
IN YOU I remain.

All This Time (The Book in Your Hands)

All this time
You held the book in Your hands
Then You didn't edit
You stuck with the plan

Here am I
Still picking up the pieces
Wondering how the world
Keeps turning

I'm back here again

Back to feeling like
There's nothing more to me
Than a girl who's fallen down
Who's stumbled many times
And somehow landed on grace

All this time
I've heard my mind turn to questions

I even hated myself
For wondering if You're there
I found no answers
And drew my own conclusions
Maybe I gave up
Or that You just turned away

Why am I so afraid
To admit that I'm confused?
To face the fact that I never
Gave all that I am to You?

Yes, I am afraid
Afraid to be real
Afraid to let anybody into my world
Afraid that they would judge
The cynic inside of me
As hard as I am
On that part of myself
Some days

So what?
What if I stood in the rain
And let You wash me clean?
What if I stepped onto the water
And You held me up?

What if I admitted
It's hard to let You in,

But I left the door unlocked
And You walked in anyway?

All this time
I've been holding on
But mostly on to being afraid
And it's the parts I never gave to You
That now stare me in the face

Journey of a Thousand Miles

It seemed like a thousand miles
From her sixth birthday
To her twentieth year
All her scars
Mark the forest paths
Can't turn back
Now that she's here

Keep moving forward
One foot at a time
After standing still
Feeling paralyzed

So many wishes
So many tears
So little time
So many fears
Hidden to the world

Insecurities make her wonder why
She keeps to herself
All the things that could have been different

If she had asked for help

Caught in the same familiar battles
Learning to find strength within
She closes her eyes
Feels the doubt start to rattle
In the fury of the wind

Letting go is how it all begins

Turned around
Changed from inside-out
Can't believe how she used to be
And how she looks now
Never knew life could be so cruel
Or taste so sweet
Another day, another duel
But she's still on her feet

Finally the feeling
Of coming full-circle
She's ready to take on this world
With God on her side

The Rest of Your Life (This is the Start)

Staring at the mirror before me
Looking over and over
At the girl that I see
Wondering how this all came to be
The girl staring back
She shares my name
But she's covered with change

Faced with a world
That never stays the same
It's catching up with me

Strengthened mind and tested will
Victory and heartache instilled
I guess I'm a woman now

And still, at times
I feel like a little girl
Pushed into the real world:

Do I have what it takes?
Can I really make it?

Searching inside and out
Refuse to surrender to doubt
And this face I see
Deep inside, she's still me

Rites of passage
Coming of age
Staring at a blank page
How will it read?

Welcome to the rest of your life
Most of it still hangs in the balance
Cherish every moment
Of what you can't see
Embrace every challenge

No playing games
No looking back
This is the start of the real thing

You can be anything you want to be
It's your life

Through His Eyes

I watched the sunset
On a clear night
Through His eyes
He wasn't done yet
And I awaited the sunrise

The Lord can work miracles
In an instant, you see
He is such a wonder
I wonder what He sees in me
The most powerful, glorious One to be

I cannot do that
My heart is much too weak
And His
Oh, His is strong
Too shy to speak
And knowing much too wrong
His reign will be forever
Forever is long
Surely I cannot do that

But when I feel I can do no more
His presence inspires me
The urging never a bore

From the Man who calmed the sea

For once you have your heart in His
It shall never fully break
If there is someone that you miss
A comfort He will make

All through His eyes

Time and Life --
Lost in the Hours

Time and life
Remain intertwined
Seems I'm always waiting it out
Tomorrow gets cluttered
Inside my mind
It's all I can think about

And just getting through
Is my ambition
Can't I ever enjoy today?
It puts me in a tight position
In a box --
I can't get away

Do you ever feel lost in the hours?
The minutes ticking by
So slowly

Ever get carried away by the power
Of the endless cycle
That leaves you lonely?

You wish you could fix time
To suit you
But we're living under rules
That aren't our own
A greater plan
We have yet to be shown

I wish I could get yesterday
Out of my head
All the dumb mistakes I made
All the useless words I said

And I wish I could be so strong
Go back and right every wrong
But I know I have to live
Where I stand
I can't change what I've done
Or where I've been

And I now feel washed in the hours
The minutes that go by
So fast

I'm carried away by the power
Of careless words
And causing hurt
That seems to last

I wish I could fix time

To fix me
But we're living under rules
That aren't our own
A greater plan
We have yet to be shown

Walk Through

Sometimes it's hard to believe
This road is where
Life has taken me
Some days
Just don't seem real
I turn around
To question what I feel

Bound by the rules of time
Maybe tomorrow
I will get it right

Feels like
Every day is just a walk-through
With all the things I never
Bring myself to do
Half-expecting encounters
That slipped through my hands
To walk back in the door
And I'll get another chance

Oh, there's so much I have seen
Hit again by reality
And life leaves no time

For a redo
So I look ahead and
Continue to walk through

For My Life

I don't know
Where these words come from
They just pour out
I only know
You're God's Holy Son
And with a mighty SHOUT

You shook the ground beneath my feet
Shattered my heart as I knew it
Now I know that
From my first heartbeat
We've been a perfect fit

And I can tell You anything
You'll still love me the same
I can't imagine
You'd even care to know my name

So thank You, Lord
I forget to say
I'm so grateful You love me
Thanks for the hope
That won't fade away
And always thinking of me

Thank You for life
Thank You for my life

My heart spills over
With words to say
My mind still wonders how
You could see me through
Day after day
And still love me somehow

My life is worth nothing
If not given to You
In everything I say and do
You show me a better way

And I
Thank You, Lord
I forget to say
I'm so grateful You love me
Thanks for the hope
That won't fade away
And always thinking of me

Thank You for life
Thank You for my life

Oh, thank You for my life

I Danced

The clouds roll in
The sun disappears
The dark of sin
Grows nearer and nearer

Shadows loom
Stretching longer still
Rumbles roll
Echo from the hills

Soon it thunders
But I'm not scared now
Raindrops strewn
Puddles laid down

Rainbow of glory comes
Without a hitch
It's all I needed
That simple first pitch

And I danced
In the rain of His love
Happy again
Feeling like a child
Danced in the rain of His love

Fiercely tamed
Taken from the wild

Feeling the joy from above
Eager to dive into this chance

I danced

Oh My Adonai

Singing, "Holy, Holy, Holy"
Never sounded so sweet
Where once I was lonely
Now I bow at Your feet

Lord, I don't know
Why You love me
But I believe that You do
I find myself
Down on my knees
To sing something for You

When I look around me
I am amazed
At such a God
Who will never change
Now, I believe it
But I'm still blown away

Oh my Adonai
Lord Most High
My heart sings Your praise
Humble my heart before Your Holy eyes
Light my spirit ablaze
As I lift to You

This rising cry
Oh my Adonai

So I won't fear
The end of the earth
I won't fret
The not-yet-known
From the moment of my birth
Lord, You have always shown

Yes, You've shown me

You'll carry me again and again
I need only trust in Your plan
I know it's You
I'm holding on to

You're here in my heart
You're all around
We're never apart
I won't crash down

And that amazes me

Adonai, Lord Most High
My heart sings Your praise
I'm humbled by
The love in Your eyes
Light this holy flame

May You hear my cry
Oh my Adonai

You are my Savior
Forever

Holy Lord
Exalted in the highest

My Adonai

Psalms 18 and 27

Set my feet
High upon a rock
When the day of trial comes
Let me rest
In the shelter of Your wings
When I fade
And my heart succumbs

To the things of this world
That don't make sense
Make me feel overtaken
Each day finds me worried and tense
But in You
My soul is awakened

The LORD lives!
Praise be to my Rock!
Exalted be God my Savior!
The LORD lives!
Praise be to my Rock!
Exalted be God my Savior!

The God who avenges me
Fights off my enemies
Raises me

To sit at His feet

I take refuge in You, my God
May I not be put to shame
In Your tent
I lift shouts of joy
Singing praises to Your Name

I will see Your goodness
In this I am secure
All Your ways are perfect
And Your Word is pure

The LORD lives!
Praise be to my Rock!
Exalted be God my Savior!
The LORD lives!
Praise be to my Rock!
Exalted be God my Savior!

My God who won't fade in sleep
Who will draw me from the deep
Your face, Oh Lord, will I seek

Everything I Am

You are my rock and my salvation
I shall not be moved
You are my Lord
Forevermore
And I shall not be moved

You've brought me too far
To back down here
I'm letting go of this world
Releasing my fear

Your Word is written on my heart
So I can read it
You've lit a fire in my soul
Help me feed it
Every part of me
Is filled with You
Can't they see?
You're everything I am

I've found my life
And now I'm free
Your love is all I see
I'm trusting You
I am strong when I am weak

When I don't think I can speak
I turn to You

Maybe I don't understand
But I'll follow anyway
I'll reach out for Your hand
And let You lead the way

Your Word is written on my heart
So I can read it
You've lit a fire in my soul
Help me feed it
Every part of me
Is filled with You
Can't they see?
You're everything I am

I've found my life in You
You're gonna see me through
You know me inside out
You're what my world's about

In my every thought
In the darkest room
Through a lonely night
You remain my
Holy, Almighty, Everlasting Light
A candle burning bright
Inside of me

Every part of me
Is filled with You
Can't they see?
You're everything I am

March On, Sister (Our Sound)

I'm not trying
To start a revolution.
I only want to see a better world.
And I'm aching
To find a real solution.
We're all looking for
A reason to believe.

It's curious to me:
What will be the call to action?
The links within a chain --
We could cause a chain reaction.

Are you with me?

If we won't be moved,
Then it's time to get a move on!

Strike while the iron is hot!
You can only give what you've got!
Surely it won't be enough
To turn the world around,

But we're makin' waves
With our sound!

So
March on, my sister!
Bang it on that drum!
Dance to your own rhythm.
Sing it out or hum.

And the world will hear our melody.
They'll have to play our song.
A force too great to be ignored!
A thunderclap too strong!

BANG!
Stomp it out!
Let's stomp it now!
Every beat of your heart.
Step it right.
A right-left-right!
We'll launch it off the charts!
Send the message
Louder still!
A joyful noise
An iron will

An army near 4 billion,
We've made our presence known.
Keep shining in the shadows.

Don't settle for one zone!

Your "place" is all around you,
The light is in your eyes.
So speak it all the louder,
And may the Truth arise!

Not afraid to look behind us.
It tells us where we've been.
Yet we trudge on toward tomorrow,
For a higher cause. Amen!

Until All Believe

I want to sing a song
That will be sung for generations
To worship Your Name
Until all believe
In every nation

Then we'll sing in one voice
Exalt and rejoice
Acclaim You as King
Have Your way in everything

I want to write the words
That reflect Your heart
To echo the truth, but
Before I start

May my mind be right with You
And Your wisdom guide me through
That the seeking soul would hear
The Good News loud and clear

Until all believe
I'm standing strong
With an undying love for You
Until You return

To right all wrongs
The workers here are few

I know You reward the faithful
Someday I'll receive my crown
But in this world
I'm called to concede
My life to You
Until all believe

My heart, my soul, my all
For You, my risen Lord
Light within the darkness
We stand upon Your Word

May it ring out all the louder
To the corners of the earth
The song of our salvation
Let us speak to what You're worth

He calls us out
To every place
The faithful ones
Who seek His face
We testify
Amazing grace
How sweet the sound!

Until every knee bows

Until all believe

Calm Before the Storm

The day was just beginning
I watched the people swarm
But this was just
The calm before the storm

Life went on
As it always would
Like everyone forgot
Amazing
How they all could
But only I did not

The calm was silent
Full of peace
No one could see through
Somehow suspense did not cease
And only I knew

What danger lay in store
Why we should be aware
You didn't bother

To preach to the few
I didn't even dare

They laugh and point
And force you out
The reception isn't warm

Its bending joint
The winding route
The calm before the storm

Rise and Fall (Petals of a Rose)

This time of year
My heart feels unsettled
I know it's impossible to come home
Life anchors me here

September
Used to seem so far away
But the last month
Knocked us flat
Took all our breath away
Summer never lasts forever

With the changing of the seasons
My spirits rise
And fall
Like the petals of a rose
Whose beauty
The world will never know

And maybe
That flower is me
Where are my roots?

Where is my color?
And why doesn't anyone see
The beauty I know is inside?

Sometimes I think
I'll always be
Trapped inside the ghosts
Of my broken dreams
Wishing my rose hadn't faded
As my heart aches for a haven

For all I've lost
The pieces I've picked up
And the ones
I won't get back
My heart searches still
Longing to be home

Closer to Goodbye

The miles roll by
Distance, space and time
And when I stop to add it up
At long last, I find
I've been nowhere
All I've really been is nowhere

That's how a month goes by
That's how I lose another
Year of my life
Measuring
By what I hold in my hands
Living in the moment
Then it's gone

All these years
The knowledge gained
Countless tears
Sleepless nights
The dreams inside of me
Can't erase
Won't replace
What I thought I wanted
Where I thought I'd be

'Cause everything
Soon becomes a memory
For better and for worse
From days you wish would never end
To the times you'd
Just as soon forget

Seasons change without warning
The best of times
Is as good as yesterday

When I think about
Those summers that we knew
It seems the older I got
The quicker they were through
To think that they say,
"Breeze on by"
To describe the summertime...
A lot of reminiscing
Takes us back to Junes

So hold on tight
These are the days
That are gonna fly
Summer to Christmas
In the blink of an eye
Then back again
To July

There's no use in holding on
It will slip right through your hands
In the end

Every chance
We get to take in this life
Every road
Will one day lead to goodbye
Oh, I know that I
Could close my eyes
And continue to pretend
But the fact remains
With each passing day
I'm only getting closer to the end

In the End

When you're trapped inside
The fury of the wind
Your energy is fading
You struggle just to bend
Remember I'm on your side
When it keeps you up at night

Close your eyes
And I'll be there
Holding you close to me
Until you find relief
I'm with you in the end

When the rain keeps driving hard
Pounding 'gainst the pavement
To match the pounding
Of your heart
No trace of sunshine peeking through
Feels like it's falling on only you
'Cause no one else
Is coming apart

Come
Seek the shelter of my arms
Runaway

Call me your escape
We'll get through another day
I'll be with you at the end

Neither one knows
What lies down the road
We're standing here at the start
Right now the appeal
Is in how it feels
To have a place to fall apart

Look in my eyes
And just believe
Forget the world
And start to breathe

When the city's rushing by you
Like the world left you behind
Feels like you're sifting through
The darkness of your mind
When loneliness calls out your name
And every day
Is just more of the same

Reach for me
You know I'm never far
You have no idea
What I would give
To get to where you are

It feels like a world away
Some days
But I promise
I'll be there for you
Some way

So when the night comes closing in
To watch you fade away again
I'll be there in the end

Don't let this life steal your dreams
You have to know that it won't win
'Cause I'll be there in the end

9 789357 447591